P9-DMI-905

BOOK THREE

WALKING WITH CHRIST

NAVPRESS
Bringing Truth to Life
P.O. Box 35001, Colorado Springs, Colorado 80935

Our Guarantee to You

We believe so strongly in the message of our books that we are making this quality guarantee to you. If for any reason you are disappointed with the content of this book, return the title page to us with your name and address and we will refund to you the list price of the book. To help us serve you better, please briefly describe why you were disappointed. Mail your refund request to: NavPress, P.O. Box 35002, Colorado Springs, CO 80935.

The Navigators is an international Christian organization. Our mission is to reach, disciple, and equip people to know Christ and to make Him known through successive generations. We envision multitudes of diverse people in the United States and every other nation who have a passionate love for Christ, live a lifestyle of sharing Christ's love, and multiply spiritual laborers among those without Christ.

NavPress is the publishing ministry of The Navigators. NavPress publications help believers learn biblical truth and apply what they learn to their lives and ministries. Our mission is to stimulate spiritual formation among our readers.

© 1973 by The Navigators
Revised edition © 1980
All rights reserved. No part of this publication may be reproduced in any form without written permission from NavPress, P.O. Box 35001, Colorado Springs, CO 80935.
www.navpress.com

ISBN 08910-9038X

Scripture quotations are from the Holy Bible: New International Version® (NIV®). Copyright © 1973, 1978, 1984 by International Bible Society. Used by permission of Zondervan Bible Publishers.

Printed in the United States of America

31 32 33 34 35 36 37 38 / 08 07 06 05 04 03

FOR A FREE CATALOG OF
NAVPRESS BOOKS & BIBLE STUDIES,
CALL 1-800-366-7788 (USA)
OR 1-416-499-4615 (CANADA)

GETTING THE MOST FROM YOUR STUDY

The Bible is a book of life, a treasure chest of truth—

...reviving the soul,
...making wise the simple,
...giving joy to the heart,
...giving light to the eyes,
...more precious than gold,
...sweeter than honey—
and in obeying its teachings there is great reward.

—from PSALM 19:7-11

The abundant wisdom and riches God has provided in his word are available to every Christian, but they are possessed only by those who diligently seek them. Meditation and prayer are two keys which unlock this storehouse of God's wisdom as you study. Prayerfully meditating on the verses you look up will help you understand their meaning and their application for your life.

In *Walking with Christ* you will be studying five important aspects of your life with him:

- Maturing in Christ
- The Lordship of Christ
- Faith and the Promises of God
- Knowing God's Will
- Walking as a Servant

CHAPTER ONE

MATURING IN CHRIST

Today's world is characterized by many inventions which meet people's needs quickly and easily: instant foods, instant electronic communication, instant information stored in high speed computers. Christians must remember, however, that there is no such thing as "instant maturity" in the Christian experience. Becoming a Christian begins a lifelong adventure of knowing God better and loving him more.

> *"Don't let the world around you squeeze you into its own mold, but let God remake you so that your whole attitude of mind is changed. Thus you will prove in practice that the will of God is good, acceptable to him and perfect."*
>
> —ROMANS 12:2 (PHILLIPS)*

MOVING TOWARD MATURITY

1. You took your first step toward spiritual maturity when you put your faith in Christ. List here and on the next page the important points of the gospel message, with scriptural references:

____

____

____

*From *The New Testament in Modern English, Revised Edition,* © 1958, 1960, 1972 by J. B. Phillips.

2. Read Ephesians 4:11-16.

a. What is God's desire for you? *Verses 13, 15*

b. What are some characteristics of immature Christians ("children" or "infants")? *Verse 14*

c. According to this passage, what characterizes a spiritually mature person?

3. Contrast man's old nature with the Christian's new nature. *Ephesians 4:22-24*

OLD NATURE	NEW NATURE

4. Consider 2 Corinthians 3:18.

a. Into whose image are you being changed?

b. Who brings about this change?

c. Are you completely changed all at once?

5. What do the following verses in Romans tell you about your relationship to Christ?

a. What has already happened to you? *Romans 5:8-9*

b. What should you be doing now? *Romans 6:19*

c. What can you expect in the future? *Romans 8:16-18*

These three aspects of salvation in Christ are helpful in understanding God's plan for believers:

Justification	*Past* tense—I have been saved . . . from the penalty of sin.	My *position* is in Christ.
Sanctification	*Present* tense—I am being saved . . . from the power of sin.	My *condition* is becoming like Christ.
Glorification	*Future* tense—I will be saved . . .from the presence of sin.	My *expectation* is to be like Christ.

6. Think carefully about Colossians 3:2-4. How do these verses relate to the preceding chart?

YOUR STARTING POINT

7. Examine Colossians 2:6-7. How did you begin your life in Christ?

How should you continue to grow?

8. Consider Romans 5:1-5. Because of your justification by faith in Christ, what practical benefits are yours to experience?

9. Read Ephesians 1 and list several things which you have "in Christ."

THE PROCESS OF GROWTH

10. A revealing parallel exists between physical life and spiritual life. What can you learn about this parallel from the following references?

1 Thessalonians 2:11

1 Timothy 4:8

Hebrews 5:13-14 ______________________

____

1 Peter 2:2-3 ______________________

____

What other illustrations of this parallel do you know?

____

____

____

____

11. What things listed in Romans 5:17 can you receive?

____

____

What will this enable you to do? ______________________

____

12. Meditate on Romans 6:11-13.

a. What should you count as true about yourself? *Verse 11*

____

____

b. What should be your present relationship to sin? *Verse 12*

____

____

c. What must you not allow? *Verse 13*

____

____

d. What action should you take? *Verse 13*

____

e. How would you explain the truth of Romans 6:5-6?

____

____

13. God intends for you to reign in life (Romans 5:17), not for sin to reign in your life (Romans 6:13). What application do these verses suggest for your life?

____

____

____

14. Paul stated that Christians are saved through faith (Ephesians 2:8-9), but your relationship to God does not end there.

a. According to Ephesians 2:10, what are you?

____

b. Is God still working in you? ______________________________

c. What is God doing? *Philippians 1:6* ______________________________

____

As you reflect on your life, be thankful for all that God is doing in you. Conflicts in your life should encourage you because they indicate that God is still working in you, changing you to be like Christ. Take a moment to express your gratitude to God for what he *has done, is doing,* and *will do* for you.

> *Our outer person is merely God's frame—the real picture is the inner person which God, the Artist, is still creating.*

HOW TO LIVE

15. What guidelines for your life as a Christian do you see in these verses:

Romans 8:4 ______________________________

____

2 Corinthians 5:7 ______________________________

Ephesians 5:2 ______________________________

____

1 John 2:6 ______________________________

____

16. Using 1 John 1:6-10, contrast those who walk in fellowship with God and those who do not.

PEOPLE IN FELLOWSHIP WITH GOD	PEOPLE NOT IN FELLOWSHIP WITH GOD

THE MATURE LIFE

17. What attitude should a mature Christian possess? *Philippians 3:13-15*

18. Read 1 Corinthians 15:58. While awaiting eternity with Christ, what should Christians be doing?

What fact can motivate you to do this?

19. What are some areas in which you can experience spiritual growth?

2 Peter 3:18

1 John 4:16-17

20. Consider 2 Timothy 4:7-8. What statement was Paul able to make concerning his earthly walk with Christ?

____

____

What did he expectantly await in the future? ______________

____

Remember These Points:

- God intends Christians to mature and become like Jesus Christ. God has saved Christians from the penalty of sin. They are presently engaged in a conflict with sin, but can anticipate a sinless future with Christ.
- Faith in Jesus Christ marks the beginning of Christian growth. The believer has God's resources available to him to help him grow.
- Spiritual growth is similar to physical growth. It takes time as God works in the believer's life. Christians should reign in life, recognizing that God is bringing to fulfillment the work he began in them.
- Growing in Christ is similar to walking. Led by the Spirit, Christians are to walk in faith and love and in fellowship with Christ.
- A mature Christian is one who continues to follow Christ, abounding in his work and experiencing his grace and love. God does not forget the work of the believer and will one day reward him.

CHAPTER TWO

THE LORDSHIP OF CHRIST

Jesus Christ is Savior *and* Lord.

William Barclay has written, "Of all the titles of Jesus the title Lord became by far the most commonly used, widespread, and theologically important. It would hardly be going too far to say that the word Lord became a synonym for the name of Jesus."*

THE LORD JESUS CHRIST

1. Titles reveal important information about the person to whom they refer. What are Jesus Christ's titles in the following verses?

John 13:13 ______________________________

Acts 2:36 ______________________________

Revelation 19:16 ______________________________

Summarize what these titles reveal about Jesus Christ.

____

2. Jesus Christ is Lord of (connect the following answers with the corresponding references):

Creation	Colossians 1:16-17
The living and the dead	Colossians 1:18
All Christians—the church	Romans 14:9

*From *Jesus as They Saw Him* (New York: Harper and Row, 1962), page 408.

Christ should have the same place in our hearts that he holds in the universe.

3. Write your own definition of the word *lord* as you feel it applies to Jesus Christ. (A dictionary may aid you here.)

____

____

____

____

4. Examine Philippians 2:9-11.

a. How has God exalted Jesus Christ? ______________________

____

____

b. How will every person exalt him? ______________________

____

5. How do the angels acknowledge Christ's lordship in Revelation 5:11-12?

____

____

____

6. Read 1 Corinthians 6:19-20.

a. How did you become God's possession? ______________________

____

b. Therefore, what should you do? ______________________

____

____

____

Jesus Christ, Lord of lords, has always existed and always will. Not all people presently acknowledge him as their Lord, but that does not alter the fact of his lordship. All will someday acknowledge Christ as Lord, but the privilege of acknowledging and obeying his lordship is possible now. Allow Christ to be the Lord of your life—by *decision* followed by *daily practice.*

7. What place should Christ hold in a believer's life? *Colossians 1:18*

____

Christ is present in all Christians;
Christ is prominent in some Christians;
But in only a few Christians is Christ preeminent.

8. What are we commanded to do in Romans 12:1?

____

____

Why should you do this?________________________

____

____

____

9. Check any of the sentences below which apply to you.

a. I generally think or feel that. . .

___Jesus doesn't really understand my problems.

___He may want me to do something I can't.

___He may want me to enter a career which I could not enjoy.

___He will prevent me from getting married.

___He will take away my enjoyment of possessions, hobbies, or friends.

___He can help me in the "big" things, but he doesn't care about the little things.

b. Are there any other fears which have prevented you from giving Christ access to every area of your life?

____

____

c. How does the statement in Jeremiah 29:11 dispel these fears?

____

____

> *"A clear and definite activity of the will is involved in recognizing his lordship, since he is to be Lord of all. By her 'I will' the bride at the marriage altar, ideally, forever enthrones her groom in her affections. In subsequent years she lives out in detail all that was implied in that momentary act of the will. A similar enthronement of Christ can result from a similar act of the will, for the same decision as enthrones Christ automatically dethrones self."*
>
> —J. OSWALD SANDERS*

10. Consider the following questions and check the appropriate box:

	ME	JESUS
Who knows perfectly what is best for my life?	☐	☐
Who is most able to do what is best for my life?	☐	☐
Who desires at all times what is truly best for my life?	☐	☐

Why? ____________________________________

____

____

____

11. Prayerfully meditate on the lordship of Christ. Have you decided to acknowledge Jesus' lordship in your life?

YES___ NO___

Explain your answer.

____

____

*From *The Pursuit of the Holy* (Grand Rapids, Michigan: Zondervan, 1972), page 65.

ACKNOWLEDGE HIS LORDSHIP IN PRACTICE

12. Good intentions don't guarantee good results. A good start does not ensure a strong finish—decision is only the beginning. Once you have decided to acknowledge the lordship of Christ in your life, you will prove that he *is* Lord by submitting to him hour by hour and obeying him in the daily affairs of life. Some of these areas are represented in the following illustration.

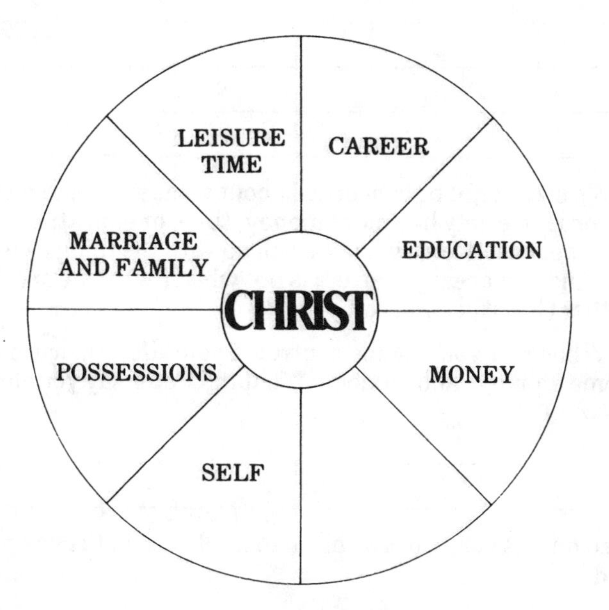

Take a few moments to evaluate your practice of the lordship of Jesus Christ in these areas. A good way to determine if Christ is in control is to ask, "Am I willing to do whatever Christ desires in this area?" or "Will I be able to thank God for whatever may happen in this area?"

a. Are there any areas in the illustration which you are not allowing Christ to control?

____

____

b. Are there other areas which you are not allowing Christ to control?

____

____

____

c. What can you do in these areas to acknowledge Christ's lordship?

____

____

____

____

____

We should not be concerned about what we would do for the Lord if we only had more money, time, or education. Instead, we must decide what we will do with the things we have now. And what really matters is not who or what we are, but whether Christ controls us.

13. Whenever you assume control of your life, you will soon become unhappy and anxious. What did Peter say you can do? *1 Peter 5:6-7*

____

____

Based on this verse, draw this man's solution in the box provided.

14. What can happen if cares and worries are not committed to Christ? *Mark 4:18-19*

How do you think this takes place?

15. In Luke 9:23, what three things is the person who decides to follow Christ called to do? (Write them in your own words.)

16. Read Colossians 3:23-24. Underline the best answer below and explain why it is better than the other two:

Paul said a Christian should:

Serve Christ more sincerely than he serves people.

Not try to mix his religion and his everyday life.

Do ordinary tasks wholeheartedly because he is really serving Christ.

17. According to Luke 6:46, what is a good way to evaluate if Christ is truly Lord of your life?

18. Read Luke 18:28-30.

a. What had the apostles done? ____________________

____

b. How did Jesus respond? ____________________

____

19. What does the lordship of Christ mean to you personally?

____

____

____

____

____

____

____

____

Remember These Points:

- Jesus Christ is declared to be Lord in the Scriptures. He is worthy to be Lord because of who he is and what he has done.
- Because Jesus Christ is Lord, the Christian's responsibility is to acknowledge his authority every day in all areas of his life.
- Various areas of a believer's life may not be subject to the control of Christ. The Christian should submit these areas to Christ and continue to recognize that Christ's control of his life is for his own welfare and joy.

CHAPTER THREE

FAITH AND THE PROMISES OF GOD

A group of people once asked Jesus how they could do the work of God. Jesus replied, "The work of God is this: to believe in the one he has sent" (John 6:29). God desires belief and faith from us, for "without faith it is impossible to please God" (Hebrews 11:6).

But often our "faith" is nothing more than wishful thinking—"I hope everything works out all right. I have 'faith' that it will." The biblical concept of faith far surpasses this superficial approach.

WALKING BY FAITH

1. How does faith relate to the *beginning* of the Christian life?
Ephesians 2:8-9

____

____

You received Christ by faith, how then should you live?
Colossians 2:6

____

____

2. How would you define faith from:

Acts 27:25 __________________________________

____

Romans 4:20-21 ______________________________

____

____

Hebrews 11:1 ______________________________

____

> *"Faith is the assurance that the thing which God has said in his word is true, and that God will act according to what he has said in his word. . . . Faith is not a matter of impressions, nor of probabilities, nor of appearances."*
>
> —GEORGE MULLER*

3. What does faith make possible? Match the following.

___Hope, joy, peace	a. *Matthew 21:22*
___Answered prayer	b. *Romans 15:13*
___Power over Satan	c. *Ephesians 3:12*
___Access to God	d. *Ephesians 6:16*

4. State the principle of 2 Corinthians 5:7 in your own words, and give an example of how you can apply it.

____

____

____

____

____

____

5. What sin can exclude you from seeing God work?
Matthew 13:58

____

> *The opposite of faith is not doubt; it is unbelief. Doubt only needs more facts. Unbelief is disobedience and refuses to act in accordance with what God has declared.*

*As quoted in *George Muller: Man of Faith* by Basil Miller (Minneapolis: Bethany Fellowship, 1972), pages 27-28.

6. What are some of the unworthy objects in which people may place their faith?

Psalm 33:16-17 ____________________

____

Psalm 146:3 ____________________

Proverbs 3:5 ____________________

Proverbs 28:26 ____________________

Jeremiah 9:23 ____________________

Place a check by those you find yourself most likely to depend on. What do you feel is the inevitable result of placing faith in these objects?

____

____

____

____

7. Who should be the object of your faith? *Mark 11:22*

____

8. Your confidence and faith in God are built on your knowledge of who God is and what he is like. What verses about God's nature and character have been significant to you?

VERSE	WHAT THIS SHOWS ME ABOUT GOD

9. Describe what the following illustration communicates.

EXAMPLES OF FAITH

10. Hebrews 11 is a key chapter on faith. Read through all of this chapter, taking note of the things accomplished by faith.

a. Which of the things accomplished by faith do you consider to be the most significant?

b. Why did you choose this? ______________________

____

____

THE PROMISES OF GOD

11. Think of a specific situation when someone promised you something.

a. How did you evaluate whether or not that person would keep his promise?

____

b. Did he keep it? ______________________

c. How does this affect your attitude toward his future promises?

____

12. God also makes certain promises to you. What does Scripture say about the words of God?

1 Kings 8:56 ______________________

____

Psalm 89:34 ______________________

____

Isaiah 55:11 ______________________

____

2 Peter 1:4 ______________________

____

13. Why do you think God's promises are trustworthy?

____

____

____

____

____

PROMISES TO CLAIM

14. Fill in the following chart.

	PROMISE	CONDITION, IF ANY
John 15:7		
Lamentations 3:22-23		
Romans 8:28		
Galatians 6:7		

15. Why do you feel God places conditions on some promises?

16. What is God's attitude about fulfilling his promises to you? *2 Corinthians 1:20*

What should your attitude be in claiming God's promises? *Hebrews 6:12*

It is helpful and encouraging to note God's promises. You may want to keep a list of these promises, their conditions, and their results. God's promises often form a "chain" like the example below.

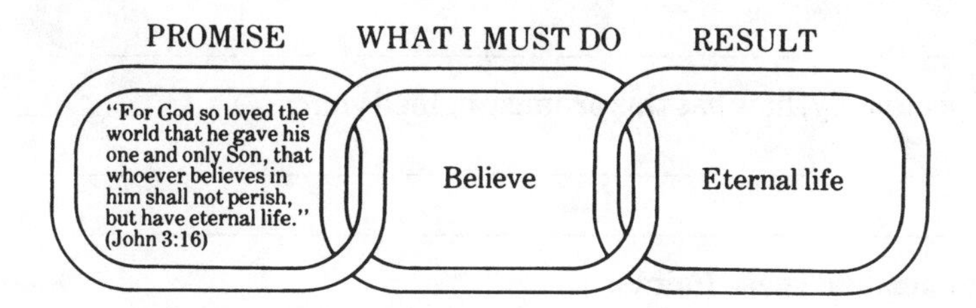

17. Discover how Jehoshaphat utilized the promises of God. Read 2 Chronicles 20:1-30.

a. What was the first thing Jehoshaphat did? *Verses 3, 6-12*

____

b. How did God answer him? *Verse 15* ______________________

____

____

c. Was this a promise? ______________________________

d. What was his next response? *Verse 18* ________________

____

e. What evidence is there that Jehoshaphat believed God's promise?

____

____

____

f. How did he encourage others? *Verse 20* ________________

____

____

g. What was the result? *Verses 22, 27* __________________

____

18. What is one promise you have discovered in your Bible reading?

___

___

___

Specifically, how has this promise helped you? ___

___

___

Remember These Points:

- Faith is based on the word of God.
- People may entrust their lives to a number of objects which will ultimately fail. The only worthy object of faith is God.
- To me, the most significant example of faith from Hebrews 11 was:

  ___

  ___

- God is a faithful Promiser whose words never fail. God does what he says he will do because he is faithful to his word.
- Christians should claim God's promises, for he desires to respond to our faith.

CHAPTER FOUR

Sometimes it may seem to you that God's will is hidden in a buried treasure chest and you have only small portions of the map to find it. But is this true? Is God keeping his plans from you as some hidden secret? Or will he allow you to follow him, and lead you step by step?

Proverbs 3:5-6 can clear up misconceptions about knowing God's will. Meditate on it carefully: "Trust in the Lord with all your heart and lean not on your own understanding; in all your ways acknowledge him, and he will make your paths straight."

THE REVEALED WILL OF GOD

1. What should be one of your desires as a follower of Christ? *Ephesians 5:17*

____

2. What does God promise you concerning his will for your life? *Psalm 32:8*

____

____

3. What does God reveal about his will for you in the following verses?

1 Thessalonians 4:3 ____________________________

____

1 Thessalonians 5:18 ______________________________

____

1 Peter 2:15 ______________________________

____

4. What was the psalmist's attitude toward God's will in Psalm 40:8?

____

What actions help produce this attitude? ______________________________

____

5. Who is your source of strength to do God's will?

Philippians 2:13 ______________________________

John 15:5 ______________________________

> *"The will of God is not like a magic package let down from heaven by a string . . . . The will of God is far more like a scroll that unrolls every day. . . . The will of God is something to be discerned and to be lived out every day of our lives. It is not something to be grasped as a package once for all. Our call, therefore, is basically not to follow a plan or a blueprint, or to go to a place or take up a work, but rather to follow the Lord Jesus Christ."*
>
> —PAUL LITTLE*

We often face decisions on issues which the Scriptures do not provide specific instructions for. In these cases, a Christian should apply the *principles* of decision-making which are contained in Scripture.

PRINCIPLES OF DECISION-MAKING

Objectives from Scripture
God has given particular commandments which can help you make decisions concerning your activities. If a particular course of action is inconsistent with the Bible, then you know it is not his will for you.

*From *Affirming the Will of God* (Downers Grove, Illinois: InterVarsity Press, 1971), page 8.

6. Using the following verses, state in your own words some of God's objectives for you. God wants you to . . .

Matthew 6:33 ____

____

Matthew 22:37-39 ____

____

Matthew 28:18-20 ____

____

1 Peter 1:15 ____

____

2 Peter 3:18 ____

____

Ask yourself some questions based on these and similar verses to determine your course of action:

a. Am I putting God's desire ahead of my own?
b. Will it help me to love God and others more?
c. How does this action relate to my personal involvement in fulfilling Christ's Great Commission?
d. Will this help me lead a more holy life?
e. Will this course of action increase my personal knowledge of Christ?

Honestly answering these questions will help you make a decision in accordance with God's word.

7. Using the following verses, develop questions that will help you discern God's will.

1 Corinthians 6:12 ____

____

1 Corinthians 6:19-20 ____

____

1 Corinthians 8:9 ____

____

1 Corinthians 10:31 ____

____

Obedience to God

If you refuse to obey God in what he has already shown you, why should God give you further direction? Obedience to the known will of God is important in receiving further guidance.

8. How do you gain an understanding of God's will?

Psalm 37:31 ______________________________

Psalm 119:105,130 ______________________________

9. What other action can you take to learn God's will?

Psalm 143:8 ______________________________

James 1:5 ______________________________

10. Psalm 25:4-5 is a prayer of David concerning God's direction for his life. Write this prayer in your own words, and use it now as a prayer of your own heart.

____

____

____

____

11. What conditions are given in Romans 12:1-2 for finding God's will?

____

____

____

12. Whose guidance have you been promised as you seek direction from God? *John 16:13*

____

13. Read Psalm 27:14 and Isaiah 30:18. How does "waiting on the Lord" relate to knowing God's will? How do you do it?

____

____

____

____

____

Satan rushes men—God guides them.

Openness to God's Leading

Many difficulties in determining the Lord's will are overcome when you are truly ready to do whatever his will may be.

14. You may not always know all of the possible alternatives in determining what to do. What is a means by which you can gather additional information? *Proverbs 15:22*

____

____

Counsel should be obtained from mature Christians who themselves are committed to the will of God and who know you well. It helps to talk with others who have previously made decisions in matters you are presently experiencing.

15. Explain the principle Jesus used in answering those who were questioning him. *John 7:17*

____

____

____

How does this apply to knowing God's will? ________________

____

____

____

16. When you know what God wants you to do, how should you do it? *Ephesians 6:6*

____

____

17. What are other factors that can help you discern God's leading? Match the following verses with the appropriate phrase.

___Careful and wise thinking	a. *Colossians 3:15*
___Inner spiritual peace	b. *Romans 13:1*
___Legal obligations	c. *Ephesians 5:15-17*

PRINCIPLES IN PRACTICE

18. Examine the following examples from the Bible and ask yourself these questions: What decision was made? What was the major issue in this decision?

PERSON	DECISION
Gideon *Judges 6:25-28*	________________
Moses *Hebrews 11:25-26*	________________
Demas *2 Timothy 4:10*	________________

19. The following chart may be helpful in determining God's will for a particular decision you now face.

Decision I am facing: ________________

SCRIPTURAL OBJECTIVES	YES	NO	NEUTRAL
Am I putting God's desire ahead of my own?			
Will it help me love God and others more?			
Will it help me to fulfill the Great Commission?			
Will it help me lead a more holy life?			
Will it help me further my Christian training?			

Other questions: ________________

OBEDIENCE TO GOD

Are there other areas in which I need to obey God before determining this decision?

What have I seen recently in the Scriptures that relates to this decision?

Have I prayed about this decision?

OPENNESS TO GOD'S LEADING

What are the various options I have in making this decision?

OPTIONS	ADVANTAGES	DISADVANTAGES

Am I truly willing to do whatever God wants me to?

What counsel have I received from others?

With what decision do I feel inner spiritual peace?

What circumstances relate to this decision?

CHAPTER FIVE

WALKING AS A SERVANT

Everyone enjoys being served, but few enjoy making the effort to serve others. People don't mind being *called* servants, but they do mind being *treated* as servants. The mature Christian is marked by what he will do for others without expecting anything in return.

CHRIST YOUR EXAMPLE

1. What was Christ's purpose in coming to this world? *Mark 10:45*

____

____

2. What are some ways in which Jesus served people?

Matthew 9:35 ________________________________

____

John 13:3-5 _________________________________

____

3. Read Philippians 2:5-8.

a. Whose example are you to follow? *Verse 5* __________

b. What position did Christ take? *Verse 7* ____________

____

c. How did he demonstrate his servanthood? *Verses 7-8*

____

____

____

4. Consider the command in Philippians 2:3-4.

a. What are you told to do? ______________________________

____

____

b. Can you think of any situation in which you are not practicing this attitude of living?

____

____

c. What can you *do* to correct this? ______________________________

____

____

CHRIST'S DESIRE FOR YOU

5. Read Mark 1:31.

a. After Jesus had served Peter's mother-in-law by healing her, what was her immediate response?

____

b. In what ways has Christ helped you? ______________________________

____

c. What should your response be? ______________________________

____

6. Whom should you desire to serve?

John 12:26 ______________________________

Galatians 5:13 ______________________________

Galatians 6:10 ______________________________

7. During Christ's last time with the disciples before his death, he demonstrated several things about a serving attitude. Read Luke 22:24-27.

a. What were the disciples arguing about? *Verse 24*

b. How did Jesus demonstrate his humility? *Verse 27*

c. How should Christ's followers conduct themselves? *Verse 26*

d. How is this contrary to the way the "world" operates? *Verse 25*

8. The incident in John 13:1-15 reveals much about Jesus' attitude in serving. List several lessons you can learn from this passage.

GIVING YOURSELF

Christians have been set free in Christ—not to do whatever they please, but to serve. Believers have been set free from sin to serve righteousness (Romans 6:18-19), set free from Satan to serve God (1 Peter 2:16), and set free from self to serve others (Galatians 5:13). Christians are no longer under obligation to serve the things of the old life, but free to serve voluntarily the things of the new life.

9. What did Paul call himself? *2 Corinthians 4:5*

How did this basic attitude manifest itself?
2 Corinthians 12:15

10. List several qualities of a good servant.

This week ask someone for his definition of a Christian servant. Record his answer here:

Being Humble
11. What must you continually keep in mind? *John 13:13,16*

____

____

12. As a servant you could develop pride in your serving. What can keep you from doing this? *Luke 17:10*

____

____

Observing and Meeting the Needs of Others
13. The servant is observant. "Ears that hear and eyes that see—the Lord has made them both" (Proverbs 20:12). God intends for you to use what he has given you to listen and observe.

a. How could you become a better listener? ______________

____

____

b. How could you become a better observer? ______________

____

____

(Read Proverbs 24:30-34 for an example of a man who learned by observation.)

14. What needs of others are you aware of which you could help meet?

____

____

Read Proverbs 3:27 and 1 John 3:17. What do these verses tell you to do?

____

____

____

____

Evaluating Your Serving

15. Stop for a moment and evaluate your serving.

a. Give an example of when you served another person.

___

___

b. Can you think of an example when you failed to serve another person although you were aware of a need?

___

___

___

c. In your opinion, why did you serve one time and not the other?

___

___

___

16. Why is it important to serve in the "little" things?
Luke 16:10

___

___

___

___

A SERVANT GIVES

One of the most tangible ways to serve others is to meet their material and financial needs. If you are willing to give of that which is tangible, you will be better able to give of that which is intangible—your time, your experience, your love, your life.

17. What principles provide a foundation for New Testament giving?

2 Corinthians 8:9 ___

___

2 Corinthians 9:8 ______________________________

____

18. What promises does God make to those who give?

2 Corinthians 9:6 ______________________________

____

Philippians 4:19 ______________________________

____

19. According to the verses in the following chart, to whom should you give? For each verse can you think of a specific person to whom you could give?

	TO WHOM I SHOULD GIVE	SPECIFIC PERSON TO WHOM I CAN GIVE
Proverbs 19:17		
1 Corinthians 9:14		
Galatians 6:6		
James 2:15-16		

20. Evaluate your giving.

a. Do you have a plan? ______________________________

b. To whom are you giving presently? ______________________________

____

____

c. Do you need to change any of your giving practices?

____

If so, what will you do? ______________________________

____

____

____

Remember These Points:

- Jesus Christ was not obligated to become a servant, but he did so voluntarily, giving of himself to meet people's needs.
- Christ has helped all believers, and their response should be to serve him and to serve other Christians.
- Believers must "die to self" in order to live for others. Then we are free to be servants.
- A servant must be humble and observant in little things as well as bigger ones.
- A server is a giver—not only of himself, but also of his material and financial possessions. Each Christian should have a personal plan for financial giving based on scriptural principles.

Turn your small group from just a bunch of people to a tightly knit community.

Does your small group feel like just a bunch of people? Do you long for greater intimacy and growth?

With Pilgrimage/NavPress Small-Group Training Seminars you can turn your small group into a community of believers excited to study God's Word and apply it to their lives. With new leadership skills and practical "how to" help, you'll be equipped to provide well-trained leadership and direction for your group, turning it from just a bunch of people to a community that supports and cares for one another.

Here's what you'll learn.

You'll learn ►how trends within society set the stage for small groups ►how you can use the four primary phases of group development to guarantee the right fit for every small-group member ►seven ways to cultivate a caring atmosphere ►five common problems to avoid ►the six foundational elements of every small group ►and much, much more!

Space is limited. Call (800) GRPS-R-US today for more information about seminars in your area.

(800) 477-7787, ask for offer **#303**

PILGRIMAGE
NAVPRESS
www.navpress.com

WE HAVE A STUDY THAT'S RIGHT FOR YOU.

Whether you're a new believer wanting to know the basics of Christianity, a small-group leader building new groups, or someone digging deeper into God's Word, we have something for you!

From topical to inductive, NavPress studies emphasize in-depth spiritual change for believers at all levels. Each contains a combination of questions, tools, Scripture, leader's guides, and other materials for groups or individuals. If you want to study a book of the Bible, learn to handle stress, be a good parent, or communicate effectively with God, we have the resources for your Bible study needs.

Why go anywhere else?

Call 1-800-366-7788 for more information. Ask for a FREE NavPress catalog. Log on to www.navpress.com for information, downloadable chapters, and special offers.